The countries of the European Community (EC) decided to build their future together after centuries of costly warfare. The 12 member states are: Belgium, Denmark, the Federal Republic of Germany, France, Greece, Ireland, Italy, Luxembourg, the Netherlands, Portugal, Spain and the United Kingdom. The EC countries are all welfare capitalist democracies. Democracy means that the countries are governed by elected national parliaments accountable to the voter. More than one party contests elections. Each member state also sends representatives to a European parliament in Brussels to which a 17-man Commission is answerable. The Commission in turn passes proposals to a council of ministers which passes laws for the community. Each country, however, retains its own system of justice for internal matters. All EC countries favour free enterprise, but the state takes care of many social needs. One of the aims of the Maastricht treaty which was drawn up in Feb 1991, is to make this European parliament more accountable to its electors.

The Maastricht treaty which also aims to achieve European Union amongst the 12 members, was initially rejected by the Danes in a referendum. However, at the Edinburgh summit in December 1992, an opt-out clause for Denmark on the issues of a single currency and common defense left the Danish government feeling confident that the treaty could be ratified a second time around. From 1st January 1993, the EC has also agreed to operate a single market within which goods, people, services and money can freely move.

The EC countries have a combined population of 340 million, compared with the United States' 240 million and the Former Soviet Union (FSU)'s 283 million. The 12 members occupy the western edge of the continental land mass of Eurasia, bounded by the Atlantic Ocean to the west and the Mediterranean Sea to the south. The EC countries have a tradition of monarchy as well as empire – 6 out of the 12 still have a reigning monarch. Many languages are spoken throughout Europe though they are all derived from one prehistoric tongue, called Indo-European. Many European countries outside the EC, including many previously excluded from the mainstream European life by communist domination in the years of the Cold War, now wish to join. The present 12 members are faced with a dilemma: to deepen their relationship or widen the community to embrace fellow-Europeans who share so much of their history and civilization.

A brief history of Europe

The development of a sense of Europe started with the Roman Empire. It became fractured as nation states began to evolve in the 15th century. The struggle between Germany and France dominated Europe for centuries and culminated in two world wars.

Each of the 12 member states of the European Community has its own distinctive history and culture. But these European countries have a lot in common. Geographically, of course, they share the same sector of the globe. Culturally, too, they incorporate to a greater or lesser extent the common elements of Western civilisation. There is such a thing as "European-ness". If a European were dropped into another town in Europe he or she would know how to get around. It has something to do with the layout – there is usually a church, or town hall, and streets radiating from the old centre, shops and cafes where people walk and talk all day long and late into the night.

Most European countries share the artistic and intellectual heritage of Greece and Rome, Christianity, the Renaissance of learning and the development of humanism, the effects of the religious Reformation, foreign conquests and the making and losing of empires, pioneering science and technology and the long practice of capitalism and democracy.

△ The Parthenon in Athens is a great monument of Greek civilisation. Modern architects still draw inspiration from Ancient Greek ideas.

THE NEW EUROPE:
MAASTRICHT AND BEYOND

ELIZABETH ROBERTS

A GLOUCESTER PRESS BOOK

Contents

Chapter One
A brief history of Europe————————p 4

This chapter gives an account of the history of Europe, which led up to the founding of the European Community.

Chapter Two
The community is born————————p 16

This outlines the setting up of the community. It explains the relations between the different countries.

Chapter Three
Deadline 1993————————p 20

This explains what is meant by the single European market and how it will affect the rest of the world.

Factfile 1
The European Community————————p 28

Factfile 2
The EC economy————————p 30

Factfile 3
The Maastricht Treaty————————p 31

Factfile 4
The EC administration————————p 32

Chronology————————p 34

Glossary————————p 35

Index————————p 36

▷ The Treaty of Maastricht, designed to establish ever closer European political and monetary union, was agreed at a European Community (EC) summit 9th-10th December 1991, subject to unanimous ratification by all 12 member states. The Danes voted "No", throwing this process into turmoil. The French, however, voted "Yes", and here Parisians celebrate by waving flags and dancing on the Champs Elysées.

The heritage of Greece and Rome

The civilisation which developed in Greece and Italy from around the 5th century BC gave birth to Western poetry, drama, history, law, philosophy, art, science and mathematics. Greek sculpture and architecture are still regarded as models of excellence. Greek philosophical method too is still studied today as an essential tool by Western students and scholars for debating questions such as the nature of truth and beauty.

Democracy, which was first practised in Greece, is considered the fairest system of government. In a democracy, all adult citizens regularly elect members of a parliament from any number of political parties. In 5th century Greece some cities had a system known as direct democracy. The citizens would meet in the market place to discuss problems and then vote on what to do about this. However only freemen were allowed to vote – women and slaves were excluded.

The Romans extended the achievement of the Greeks by bringing the rule of law and a physically well-ordered society to much of Europe after military conquest. The Romans built great roads, bridges and aqueducts (water pipelines) and many present-day European cities are sited on Roman settlements. There are Roman remains throughout Europe – amphitheatres, temples, villas and baths.

▽ A Roman mosaic in Sicily. From central heating and interior decoration to bridges and the rule of law, the Romans left their mark on Europe.

Christianity

Christianity began to spread throughout the Roman Empire until by 300 AD (after the birth of Christ) there were Christian strongholds in France, Germany, Italy and Spain. Christianity became the official religion of the Empire in 391 and it added a vital new element to world civilisation.

The message of Christianity was that since the Son of God (Jesus Christ) had come down to Earth to save mankind, everyone could be saved. This meant that every individual life was valuable in the eyes of God. Jesus Christ taught that "the meek shall inherit the Earth" and that love should govern all human actions. It was a message of hope to all people and many were converted to it. The effect of this revolutionary creed was astonishing: it changed European art and architecture by inspiring great religious paintings, frescoes and churches, as well as choral music. It also provided a new moral framework, because Christians believed in eternal life.

△ The Emperor Charlemagne (742-814) ruled over a Christian empire which included much of modern France and Germany.

▽ By 1500 Europe was Christian. Religion gave purpose and meaning to life, a deep wellspring for a whole civilisation of arts and learning. It gave peoples from different countries a common experience.

The Dark Ages

The Roman Empire split in two and in the 5th century AD the western part fell to invading armies from the East. (The eastern part endured until 1453.) From the 5th century onwards Europe went through a period known as the Dark Ages, when learning was restricted to a few monasteries. Between the 5th and the 8th centuries, there was also a gradual shift away from the old centres of classical civilisation around the Mediterranean, north to the valley of the Rhine.

A great Christian king emerged to rule over this central (or Frankish) kingdom: his name was Charlemagne, which means Charles the Great. He was crowned Emperor in 800, and during his reign encouraged learning and spread Christianity into pagan lands. He also brought in craftsmen from Constantinople (the capital of the Eastern Roman Empire and present-day Istanbul.) They produced treasures and beautified his court at Aachen.

Meanwhile along the coast of Western Europe and as far south and east as Sicily and Kiev (in Ukraine), pagan warriors from Scandinavia, the Vikings, were looting and pillaging. Eventually, they settled in the lands they had come to sack, and their kings (called Normans – Norsemen) became Christians ruling over the various kingdoms including one which incorporated parts of both England and Western France.

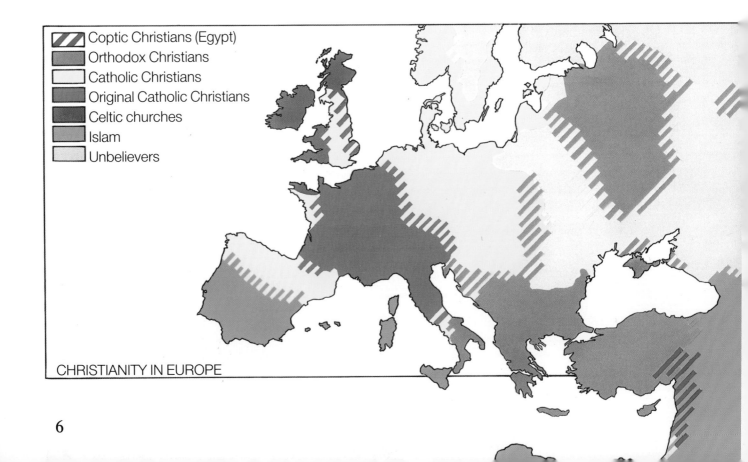

Coptic Christians (Egypt)
Orthodox Christians
Catholic Christians
Original Catholic Christians
Celtic churches
Islam
Unbelievers

CHRISTIANITY IN EUROPE

The Middle Ages

By 1500 AD most of Europe was Christian. The Church was not only the dominant spiritual force, but also enormously rich in lands and politically powerful. Enduring physical expressions of this might are the great Gothic cathedrals, such as Winchester in England and Chartres in France. Although this whole great Christian empire was in one sense ruled by the Pope as head of the Church, there were also kings and queens, dukes and duchesses ruling different countries. Among some of the people in these European countries there was a growing sense of national identity.

When the Normans had conquered England in 1066, they had kept their possessions in France. Joan of Arc (1412-1431) encouraged the French king to fight and expel the English from France. In Spain, Queen Isabella and King Ferdinand united Spain as a Christian nation when they conquered the last of the Islamic cities in Spain – Granada – in 1492. But the idea of a "nation", and a "nationality", in the sense of belonging to – and being willing to fight for – a country rather than a region or religion, is comparatively modern. Italy and Germany, for instance, were not unified into nation states until the middle of the 19th century, three or four hundred years after France and Spain. Yugoslavia and Czechoslovakia became nations for a while in the 20th century.

A new society

In the Middle Ages the feudal system, where knights and peasants were bound to work for a lord in exchange for having land, came under attack. In the towns craftsmen set up their own organisations, known as guilds, so they could obtain charters of rights and practise their trade free from the interference of the church or local nobles. These free citizens developed the traditions of honesty and public service, necessary for democracy in a modern state.

▽ Fountains Abbey was built in England by 12th century Benedictine monks. The monks took part in the wool trade, making the abbey rich.

The Age of Discovery

Throughout their history, Europeans have looked outwards to the rest of the world. The Portuguese explored the west coast of Africa and around the Cape of Good Hope across to India in the 15th century. A Genoese sea captain called Christopher Columbus tried to sail to India by going west across the Atlantic Ocean. In 1492 the words "the New World" were first used to describe his discovery of the islands of the Caribbean. These islands are known to this day as the West Indies because Columbus thought (mistakenly) that by sailing as far west as possible, he had arrived in India!

In Europe the first universities were founded as early as the 12th century. Universities were places where people could study such subjects as law, medicine and philosophy as well as theology. The Renaissance is the name given to the great flowering of learning and the arts in 15th and 16th century Europe. Printing was invented in Europe (as it had been in China many centuries before) in about 1450 by Johannes Gutenburg in Mainz. The first printed book in Europe was the Gutenburg bible in 1455. Printing speeded the transmission of ideas as more books became

△ Printing revolutionised learning and led to social change. Illustrated above is the hand-written Irish Book of Kells (top) and a Gutenburg printed page (above).

◁ The discovery of the Americas by Christopher Columbus in 1492 led to the unprecedented spread of one civilisation – the European – across the globe. This transformed the world as Europe colonised other countries to increase its wealth. Columbus' voyage had been financed by King Ferdinand and Queen Isabella of Spain.

▽ Louis XIV of France (1638-1715) provided the perfect model of the absolute ruler to other European princes. He had power over all appointments and courtiers manoeuvred for royal favour. He embarked on foreign wars and took advantage of treaties with the Dutch and British to make France the most powerful country in Europe.

available. Before printing, all books had to be individually copied by hand.

The domination of the church over all learning waned as scholars eagerly rediscovered Greek and Roman texts, love poems and early adventure stories. This non-religious learning is called Humanism because it is centred on human needs and values. Europeans also learned mathematics and medicine from their contact with Islamic countries, where these sciences were highly developed. Learned men began to question the central role of the church.

The Reformation

Modern European history begins with the Reformation – the fragmentation of Christianity from about 1517 into two strands: Protestantism and Roman Catholicism. The Protestants broke with the Pope and set up their own, often nationally based, religions. The political consequences of this break were far-reaching. The Reformation was, at the outset, an attempt to clean up corrupt practices in the Christian church, such as the encouragement to buy eternal salvation through money rather than by living a pious life. However, the effect of questioning the authority of the Pope in Rome also led in time to the questioning of the rule of the kings, whose authority was seen as divine.

The idea arose that all citizens should not only be free to practise their religious beliefs but also to have a say in the laws and people governing them. In England, when King Henry VIII chose to defy the Pope in 1531, he asked parliament to ratify his authority, thereby confirming parliament's central role in legitimate government.

In many other European countries, however, the weakening of papal rule led to the kings becoming absolute rulers. This meant that they were answerable to no one apart from – notionally – God. Following this upheaval the Catholic church fought back to re-assert itself with the Counter-Reformation. There were religious wars in many European countries. The Thirty Years' War, one result of the conflict between Protestants and Roman Catholics, left much of central Europe in ruins and the people impoverished. The Peace of Westphalia, which ended the Thirty Years' War in 1648, marked the end of the era of religious wars in Europe. For the next 150 years France was the dominant power in Europe. King Louis XIV extended France's boundaries in the north and east and despite a few defeats towards the end of his reign was able to outmanoeuvre his enemies.

The French Revolution

In the two hundred years between 1700 and 1900, the pace of political and economic change in various parts of Europe differed enormously. But a major landmark was the French Revolution in 1789. The absolute ruler, King Louis XVI, was violently overthrown. The slogan of the French revolution was "Liberty, equality, fraternity". Civil rights were now firmly on the European agenda. Further spasms of political unrest rocked the thrones of Europe in 1848, as the – eventually successful – pressure for change grew. Karl Marx, a German, published his ideas in *The Communist Manifesto*. This led to the spread of socialist ideas throughout 19th-century Europe.

Europe in the 19th century was the birthplace of scientists and thinkers whose work shaped the modern world – giants such as Charles Darwin in biology and

Citizenship
The concept of citizenship developed in Roman times. But the first modern expression of the idea that government gets its just powers from the consent of those who are governed is found in the first words of the US constitution in 1787 "We the People ...." The new French constitution in 1791 also set out the individual's rights in relation to the state.

Albert Einstein in physics. Engineers like George Stephenson with his steam locomotive made railways possible, and Europe grew rich by providing the rest of the world with ships and engines and other kinds of technology. The industrial revolution, which had started in 18th century Britain, led to demands for raw materials. These often came from the furthest parts of the globe and were processed in the mills and workshops of Europe. This resulted in a move to grab territory abroad, which gained pace in the 19th century, making European merchants and their governments rich and powerful.

△ In 1793 King Louis XVI of France was executed in the name of the people. The French Revolution occurred at a time of famine in the French countryside and complaints about high taxation in the towns. The revolution got rid of many feudal and legal inequalities but at the cost of much bloodshed (the "Terror"). Eventually Napoleon Bonaparte became military dictator and emperor.

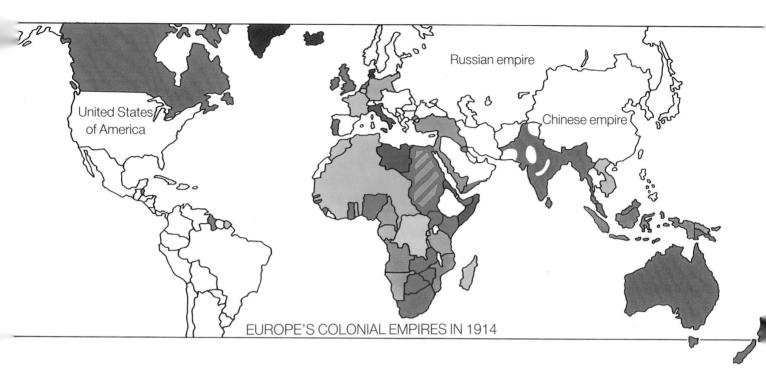

United States
of America

Russian empire

Chinese empire

EUROPE'S COLONIAL EMPIRES IN 1914

The First World War

By 1900 most of Europe was organised into nation states, vying with each other in shifting alliances for domination. War was still considered the necessary last resort to solve international disputes or gain territorial advantage. France had fought – and been defeated by – a newly-unified Germany in 1870/71.

Then, in 1914, an apparently insignificant event in a remote part of Eastern Europe plunged Europe into a great war. The assassination of Austrian Archduke Franz Ferdinand at Sarajevo the capital of Bosnia in June 1914 tripped a series of complex military alliances; and within a month the whole of Europe had mobilised. Austria-Hungary declared war on Serbia in Eastern Europe, which was allied to Russia. Germany, in alliance with Austria-Hungary, declared war on Russia. Britain and France joined Russia in a war that was supposed to last a few months but went on four long years. The casualty figures were horrifying. About nine million soldiers, sailors and airmen died. The armies fought a more or less static campaign, firing at each other from trenches.

Russia was knocked out of the war in 1917 when there was a revolution, in which the Tsar and his family were deposed and then murdered. A communist government inspired by Karl Marx's ideas swept the old order away. The German kaiser was also forced to abdicate as the German army ran out of supplies and morale. Germany signed an armistice in 1918.

- British
- French
- German
- Portuguese
- Spanish
- Dutch
- Belgian
- Italian
- Ottoman (Turkish)
- Danish
- Rest of the world

△ By 1914 four-fifths of the world was under rule by a European country. The drive for foreign conquests was not solely inspired by the greed for wealth, many Europeans thought that they would bring the benefits of their (superior they thought) civilisation to their colonies. The Europeans also exploited their colonies for their natural resources and manpower, which caused much pain and bitterness. In many former colonies these feelings are still strong.

11

The Second World War

The peace treaty signed at Versailles in 1919 after the First World War imposed heavy penalties on the Germans. This led to social and economic difficulties, and in turn to the rise of the Nazi leader, Adolf Hitler. He dragged Germany into another war. This became a global war when Japan attacked the US naval base at Pearl Harbor in December 1941. By the end of the Second World War, the European age – the age during which Europe had dominated the world – seemed over.

During the Second World War (1939-45), more than 40 million people were killed in Europe alone. The economic devastation was as great as the toll in human life. Factories and towns were destroyed, food was rationed and there was no work. In Germany in 1946, anything could be bought for a packet of cigarettes – paper money was worthless. In post-war France and Italy, governments came and went, split between squabbling factions of the right and the left. Britain, once the proud possessor of a world empire, was in colossal debt to the United States for war supplies.

△ Adolf Hitler (1889-1945) preached a dangerous mixture of racial hatred and extreme nationalism. He led Germany into the Second World War which resulted in its division.

▽ By the end of the Second World War many German cities, such as Bremen (below), were reduced to rubble by Allied aerial bombing.

Post-war Europe

During the Second World War the Soviet armies occupied vast areas of Eastern Europe including East Germany. Once the war was over, they stayed in place. Europe was now divided into democracies in the west and communist-dominated countries in the east. An "iron curtain" had fallen across Europe. Later it became known that the ruler of the Soviet Union, Josef Stalin, had caused the death of millions of Soviet citizens during his reign of terror in the 1930s and after.

Was there any way to prevent further bloodshed in Europe? This issue became even more pressing after the invention of the atomic bomb, which the United States had invented in 1945 and which the Soviet Union acquired in 1949. One man certainly thought so. Jean Monnet's idea of a European community was to bring lasting peace and prosperity to Europe through economic and political co-operation and shared institutions. He liked to quote the Swiss philosopher Henri-Frédéric Amiel: "Each man's experience starts again from the beginning. Only institutions grow wiser; they accumulate collective experience, and owing to this experience and this wisdom men subject to the same rules will not see their own nature changing, but their behaviour gradually transformed."

△ Above: Josef Stalin (1879-1953) was in command of the Soviet armed forces during the Second World War. It took four years for the Allied armies to defeat the Germans. Top: Soviet troops hand out food to Polish people in 1945. The Soviet armies remained in Eastern Europe after the war and forced those countries to accept communist governments.

Jean Monnet (1888-1979) was born in Cognac, the traditional centre of brandy-making in France. When he was a young man, Monnet travelled in the United States and Canada selling brandy. He lived in London for a while, where he learned English. He also learned the traditions of the City of London that a man's word was his bond, that is, any verbal agreement was binding. When the First World War broke out in 1914 he was 26, but he was debarred from military service on health grounds. However, he observed that the French and the British who were fighting on the same side in the war against the Germans, were duplicating much of their war effort, particularly in the use of shipping and supplies. He persuaded the authorities to appoint him co-ordinator of an Allied Supply Committee.

His success in this job led to his appointment, at the age of 31, as Deputy Secretary-General of the League of Nations, the organisation set up after the war with the goal of settling international disputes without fighting. Unfortunately, the member states were not willing to sacrifice their national interests in favour of the common good. France won heavy economic damages and territory from Germany after the First World War, which led to bitterness and political unrest in Germany and ultimately to the Second World War.

Jean Monnet left the League of Nations in 1923 to take over his family brandy business in Cognac. In 1926 he left France again, this time to set up an international commercial bank in the United States. His travels took him to Poland, Sweden and China. He advised the Polish government in Warsaw during a currency crisis. In China he met the nationalist leader, Chiang Kaishek and advised him on modernising the railways. In 1936, Monnet returned to political action, realising that another war in Europe was possible. The French Prime Minister Edouard Daladier sent him on a secret mission to the United States in 1938 to buy military aircraft. His negotiations were successful, despite the fact that at the time the United States was bound by the Neutrality Act which prohibited the export of arms to nations at war. During the early years of the Second World War several hundred American warplanes and warships were delivered to help France's ally Britain.

Throughout the Second World War, Jean Monnet was at the centre of the Allied war effort. He drafted a revolutionary Franco-British Declaration in 1940 which would have given both nations single sovereignty in the face of the impending fall of France to German troops.

▽ Jean Monnet, the father of the European Community, (in the centre of the photograph) in Luxembourg in 1952, when the European Coal and Steel Community (ECSC) was formed under his leadership. This was a practical achievement, of enormous importance because it was a revolutionary approach to international relations. The countries that joined the ECSC were giving up their sovereignty in two crucial industries to an independent authority. France had not signed a treaty with Germany at the end of the Second World War and the ECSC indicated both countries' willingness to work together peacefully in the future.

Although the declaration was nullified the following day by the new French Prime Minister, Marshal Henri Philippe Pétain who had decided to collaborate with the invader, it was a landmark in international co-operation.

After the war, Monnet was made Planning Commissioner for the French economy. However, he saw that it was necessary to include Germany in the economic recovery of Europe, and in 1950 came up with the idea of the European Coal and Steel Community. This venture was a practical, achievable step towards wider economic and political co-operation which Monnet believed was the only way to ensure peace and prosperity. Monnet remained at the centre of the European movement for the rest of his life, principally in the role of leader of the Action Committee for the United States of Europe. The action committee was an influential pressure group in support of the European ideal and allowed Monnet to spread his ideas. In 1976 he was made an "Honorary Citizen of Europe" and he died in 1979 at his home at Houjarray, outside Paris.

The future unity of Europe

Jean Monnet spoke of a "ferment of change" which he saw would be created by the European Community. Monnet had faith in the ability of Europeans to adapt and co-operate in the face of challenges. He believed any European country with a democratic system of government and which shared the desire for European union should be allowed to join the community. His motto was "Set yourself a goal and move forward by stages."

The community is born

After the Second World War France and Germany led the focus of efforts to build for a peaceful future.

The bitter aftermath of the First World War taught European statesmen that a practical effort should be made to incorporate Germany into the post-Second World War reconstruction of Europe. Also, it was clear as soon as the Second World War ended that the Soviet army would not be demobilised as most of the other Allied armies had been. After the end of the Second World War the Soviet Union had control over many countries of Eastern Europe, such as Poland, Hungary and East Germany (called, misleadingly, the German Democratic Republic), and it imposed communist governments on them.

In September 1946, Britain's wartime prime minister, Winston Churchill, made a speech in Zürich calling for the establishment of a United States of Europe. The first tentative step towards such a state was made by the French foreign minister, Robert Schuman, in 1950. He took up the idea, proposed by Jean Monnet, of a European Coal and Steel Community (ECSC). In the ECSC national governments in Western Europe were asked for the first time to delegate part of their sovereignty to a High Authority. The officials of this authority were appointed by them, but once appointed, had to act independently. The first members of the ECSC were France, the Federal Republic of Germany (West Germany), Italy, Belgium, the Netherlands and the Grand Duchy of Luxembourg.

△ The Berlin Wall was built in 1961 by the communist government of East Germany to stop the flow of refugees to the West. Anyone attempting to cross the German border at any point between east and west was shot. The Wall became the most powerful symbol of the Cold War led by the two superpowers, the Soviet Union and the United States, after the Second World War. Europe became an armed camp with massive armies stationed in both parts of Germany.

The Six

The Treaty of Paris setting up the ECSC was signed in 1951. The United Kingdom did not join the Six because it was thought that the rules were too binding, and Britain still had close trading and other links with its overseas empire, now called the British Commonwealth.

In the excitement which followed the setting up of the ECSC, politicians drew up proposals for European power-sharing in the fields of foreign affairs, defence, economic and social integration and the protection of human rights. However, hopes were dashed when the French government vetoed plans for a European army in August 1954. Instead, the Atlantic Alliance and its military organisation, the North Atlantic Treaty Organisation (NATO), which included the United States, was left with the main responsibility for defending Western Europe against the Soviet Union and its satellites in Eastern Europe. They had signed a treaty known as the Warsaw Pact, to co-ordinate their defence measures. Although France was a member of the Atlantic Alliance, it had refused to join NATO.

The Treaties of Rome

The foreign ministers of the Six met in Messina in Southern Italy in 1955, and decided to press ahead with more limited plans for European economic integration. After long debate, the Treaties of Rome was signed in 1957, establishing the European Economic Community (the EEC) and the European Atomic Energy Committee (Euratom).

▷ The Treaties of Rome, signed in 1957, set up the European Economic Community (EEC) and the European Atomic Energy Committee (Euratom). Four institutions administered these new bodies: the European Parliament, the Council, the Commission and the Court of Justice. Until 1967 the ECSC, Euratom and the EEC were all administered separately. Since then there has been a single commission and a single council.

The Treaties of Rome went further than providing for the free movement of goods between the founding six member states. They also provided for a number of common policies on matters such as agriculture, transport and foreign trade, and the harmonisation of laws on social policy and competition.

Seeing the success of the first efforts of the Six, other countries became interested in joining the community. Greece and Turkey were granted associate status as early as 1959. But a major step was the application of Ireland, Denmark and the United Kingdom to join as full members in 1961.

While their applications were still being considered, the terms of the first European Common Agricultural Policy were agreed in 1962 between the founding six member states. It was decided that farmers should be guaranteed prices for various farm goods such as grain and animal products. Many European farmers were smallholders, who had other part-time jobs. Making sure farmers had a steady income was considered essential for political reasons.

△ President Charles de Gaulle of France said "non" in 1963 to Britain's application to join the EEC. He claimed that Britain only wanted to join for economic reasons and did not support the EEC's political aims.

De Gaulle says no

In 1963 European unity suffered a setback. France's leader General Charles de Gaulle blocked Britain's application to join the community, on the grounds that he doubted Britain's commitment to Europe. Weeks later, France and Germany signed a co-operation treaty. This gesture, following so soon after France's objection to Britain's membership, dealt a severe blow not only to Britain's hopes but also, for a time, to the community itself.

△ In 1967 de Gaulle and his prime minister, Georges Pompidou, met the British prime minister, Harold Wilson, and foreign minister, George Brown. Britain had to improve its relations with other European countries before being invited to join the EEC in 1972.

△ Spanish Prime Minister Felipe Gonzales finally signed the treaty for Spain's entry into the European Community in Madrid on 12 June 1985. Portugal joined on the same day, making the community 12. They officially became members in 1986.

During the years which followed, many tense battles were fought within the community to obtain the necessary agreement between member states to allow the EEC to grow and expand. One of the most crucial issues was whether or not the community should raise its own taxes to finance its own administration. There was also a serious crisis in 1965 when General de Gaulle objected to plans to expand the community's powers and to increase majority voting in the council.

After seven months, a compromise was reached and it was agreed that whenever a member felt that its "vital interests" were at stake, the council would try to agree on a unanimous solution. However, there was no magic formula in the case of the council's failure to do so. The United Kingdom applied to join again in 1967, and again its application was vetoed by General de Gaulle. Despite the general's objections, the community gained financial autonomy – that is, the right to raise taxes and decide how to spend money – in 1970, to be supervised by a strengthened European parliament. This met the basic democratic requirement of "no taxation without representation" and also took the community a small step towards political union.

Enlarging the community
De Gaulle resigned in 1969 and eventually in 1972, three new members joined the community: Denmark, Ireland and the United Kingdom. In 1979 direct elections were held to the European Parliament. Until then the European Parliament had been appointed by member parliaments. Henceforth Members of the European Parliament (known as MEPs) were to be elected by voters every five years. One of the qualifying aspects for membership of the community is that a country must be a democracy. Now the community itself was to be run more democratically. In 1981, Greece joined the community, followed in 1986 by Spain and Portugal, making the full total of 12.

In 1979, the European Monetary System (EMS) was set up. The EMS has four main components: a European currency unit called the ecu, an exchange-rate and information mechanism, credit facilities and transfer arrangements. A common European currency and bank have been proposed as necessary to complete the effectiveness of the community in world trade. However it has been difficult to operate the EMS in practise and the United Kingdom and Italy left the EMS in 1992.

Deadline 1993

In 1986, the 12 member states of the European Community (EC) signed the Single European Act binding them to create a truly unified market within the EC by 1993. The collapse of communism in Russia and Central and Eastern Europe after 1989 placed a question mark over previously agreed goals.

The Single European Act, signed in 1986, committed the 12 to establish an area without internal frontiers by 1st Jan 1993. This means there is now a fully free movement of "goods, persons, services and capital" within the community. This apparently simple goal involves over 600 individual measures to harmonise European standards in fields as diverse as trading practices, manufacturing standards, educational qualifications and broadcasting.

The purely material potential gains for all Europeans of belonging to one community have been predicted as follows: the removal of direct frontier and other customs costs due to, for example, the waiting time for lorries and trains at the present frontiers: 9 billion ecus; savings in industrial costs because of the abolition of conflicting technical standards: 40 billion ecus; intensified competition for public purchasing – such items as street lighting, roads and school equipment: 40 billion ecus; the rationalisation of industry, whereby firms join up together to enlarge their

△ The European Commission in session. It proposes new laws to the European Council of Ministers. Under the Single European Act, a new co-operation procedure has been introduced giving the European Parliament a say on commission proposals.

▷ A car assembly line in Milan. European production facilities such as this ultra-modern robot line making luxury Alfa Romeo cars will save billions of ecus with the creation of the 1993 Single Market.

product lines and make their sales forces more effective: 60 billion ecus; the intensification of competition generally, encouraging the growth of new small businesses: 140 billion ecus. At the present time the ecu is worth about 60 pence.

European procedures

Under the Single European Act a new co-operation procedure has been introduced giving an additional say to parliament. Parliament can now give an opinion both on commission proposals and – for the first time – on the common position of the Council of Ministers. The European Parliament also has a series of specialist committees, divided by subject area. These committees examine commission proposals on agriculture, the community budget, foreign affairs, industry and so on before they are presented to parliament as a whole.

The last word on community law rests with the council. In the Council an increasing number of issues can be dealt with by a "qualified majority vote". In this type of case, Germany, France, Italy and the United Kingdom have ten votes each, Spain has eight; Belgium, Greece, the Netherlands and Portugal five each, Denmark and Ireland three each and Luxembourg two. Other issues can be dealt with by simple majority voting – that is, seven of the 12 members in favour.

Eastern Europe

In October 1989 Hungary declared itself to be no longer a "socialist republic", but simply a democratic republic in which parties could contest free elections and the Communist Party – forcibly maintained in power by Soviet tanks – was to lose its "leading role".

Also in 1989 in Poland, the reforming Catholic workers' party, *Solidarnosc* (Solidarity), under the leadership of Lech Walesa, succeeded in wresting a power-sharing deal following an overwhelming victory in the elections over the ruling Communist Party and the promise of totally free elections in due course.

Even more astonishing changes occurred in Czechoslovakia, where, over a period of ten days in November 1989, massive demonstrations and strikes led to the resignation of the hard-line communist government and later on the election of a non-communist president, the playwright Vaclav Havel. In December 1989, after 10 days of fighting when thousands died, an internal coup ended the communist tyranny of Nicolae Ceausescu and his wife Elena. Mikhail Gorbachev's policy of "glasnost" or openness in the Soviet Union led to movements for independence from central government. In 1991 the 15 republics held their first free elections and Boris Yeltsin became the new president of Russia.

The leaders of the European Community met in a hurried session to discuss what their response should be to these unexpected and sudden changes. They agreed to a massive package of economic aid both to the former Soviet Union and Eastern Europe.

△ Lech Walesa is the leader of the Polish reforming Catholic workers' party, called *Solidarnosc*. It defeated the communists in elections in 1989.

▽ Food queues and shortages are a problem in the former Soviet Union. As well as economic problems, the former Soviet Union faces internal pressures, such as, ethnic violence between Armenians and Azerbaijanis.

Rocking the Boat

The original purpose of the community was to cement together "in ever closer union" through shared wealth and institutions, a group of western European democracies. Today, these 12 are facing a period of rapid and unexpected change. The old enemy, communism, has failed. The Cold War has ended. The former Russian Empire has collapsed and with it her domination of Eastern Europe. For a generation, the so-called German question, including the post-Second World War partition of Germany, was on the back burner, so to speak. Now, Germany is unified. All the European countries previously under communist domination, including Russia, are attempting to establish free market economies and democratic governments. Many, including Russia, have expressed a desire to be considered for eventual membership of the EC. The downside to the removal of communist power is the re-emergence of inter-ethnic strife. A civil war is raging on the borders of the EC in the countries which used to make up Yugoslavia. Economic and political refugees are threatening the political stability of Italy and Germany. In 1992 alone, over 250,000 people applied for asylum in Germany – more than in the whole of the rest of the EC. Neo-fascist groups have begun to threaten foreign workers by attacking and burning down the hostels they live in. Traditional fears of the potentially destabilising power of a strong Germany are only matched – ironically – by fears of an ecomically weak and politically unstable Germany – up to now the solid financial engineroom of the community. French voters narrowly supported the ratification of the

△ Russian President Boris Yeltsin came to power in 1991. He faced the problems of a country in transition from communism to democracy.

▽ The growing violence against foreign immigrants in Germany inspired this anti-racism march in Hamburg.

Maastricht Treaty, but the French farmers are passionately opposed to the removal of direct community subsidies for agriculture. The General Agreement on Tariffs and Trade (GATT) talks have promised to yield billion-dollar benefits world-wide, but EC policies have been based on using German, English and French funds to bribe country people to stay on the land.

One organisation which bridges the gap between the EC and her European neighbours is the Council of Europe, based in Strasbourg. Hungary, Bulgaria, Poland and Czechoslovakia have all joined this first post World War II international organisation which exists to protect human rights, promote social, economic and cultural development backed by a Court of Human Rights and a Commission. Russia has applied to join, supported by France.

Relations with the rest of Europe

The first step to enlarge the European Community is envisaged via the European Economic Area (EEA). This is a free-trade zone of nearly 400 million people stretching from the Arctic to the Mediterranean. The EEA would provide for the free movement of goods, people, services and money between the 12 EC countries and the European Free Trade Association (EFTA) countries. EFTA members include: Iceland, Lichenstein, Austria, Sweden, Norway, Finland and Switzerland. Switzerland, however, voted to reject membership of the EEA on December 6 1992. A narrow majority voted against Swiss participation in the initiative created on Jan 1 1993.

◁ An aerial view of the French end of the tunnel being built to link Britain and France in 1993. If trade between European countries is to grow, then the community needs rapid, barrier-free transport. The tunnel will speed up the journey from the rest of Europe to Britain and cut down Britain's feeling of being separate from the continent. Critics of Britain's attitude to Europe point out that Britain has been extremely slow about deciding on where to route a rail link from the tunnel to London.

△ Bananas from the Windward Islands in the Caribbean are unloaded in Wales. Under the terms of the proposed new GATT agreement, producers in small countries were threatened with extinction but cheaper, competing imports are now to be limited.

Outside Europe

The community has had ties with countries outside Europe since 1963, when Turkey was welcomed as an associate member, and the first Yaoundé Convention was signed between the community and 17 African countries.

Later, the Lomé Convention (1975) provided for commercial co-operation between the community and 46 countries of Africa, the Caribbean and the Pacific (ACP). In 1979 a second Lomé Convention was signed with 66 ACP countries. Virtually all products originating from the ACP countries have free access to the community market, and the convention guarantees those countries stable export earnings from 36 basic commodities such as coffee and sugar. Third World countries are thus shielded from the ups and downs of the prices fetched by their produce on world markets. The Lomé Convention also provides for industrial co-operation between the community and the ACP countries through joint institutions in which both parties have their say on the way things are done. In 1992, the Lomé convention countries numbered 69.

In 1975, the community signed a similar agreement with Israel. In 1976, an agreement was made with the countries of the Maghreb (Tunisia, Algeria and Morocco) and of the Mashrea (Egypt, Syria, Jordan and Lebanon).

The European Community is aware of the needs of the Third World, to which it owes much of the prosperity of the last 200 years. Cheap raw materials and agricultural products helped Europe industrialise in the 19th and 20th centuries. Aid from Europe to the developing countries is aimed primarily at enabling them to take on responsibility for their own development. The average income of a person in the Third World is 920 ecus compared with 9,300 ecus of someone in Western Europe – ten times less.

Aid from the community runs at about 0.3 per cent of the Gross National Product (GNP or total income) of the community, or some 36,000 million ecus. Third World countries are crippled by debt, amounting to almost half their annual GNP. Despite the EC contribution, which has risen in real terms every year since 1975, aid is only managing to keep up with the needs of the poor in Africa and Asia, since a growing population makes ever-increasing demands on resources. Occasionally there are acute crises, such as the famines in Ethiopia. In cases such as these, when four million people were suddenly known to be at risk, the European Community made an instant contribution of money and materials.

Europe and the United States

Since the end of the Second World War, the United States has taken great responsibility for the security and prosperity of Western Europe. Now, thanks to the momentous changes in Eastern Europe, it looks as if that responsibility will diminish and change.

At the end of the war in 1945, the United States provided economic aid to a battered and broke Western Europe through the Marshall Plan. Later, by joining with 15 other countries in the North Atlantic Treaty Organisation (NATO), the United States provided massive military resources in Western Europe to contain the threat of communist expansion.

For the time being and according to the Treaties of Rome, national security is not a matter for the European Community. Western leaders have agreed that the instability caused by the great melting of the icepack in Eastern Europe makes the existence of NATO, backed by the United States, more necessary than ever. However both superpowers are engaged in negotiations to reduce the number of troops stationed in Europe, which would have far-reaching economic effects.

Although the United States welcomes the rapid development of the European single market, there are occasional hiccups. For example, the United States objects when European standards in meat or fruit appear to exclude American products or penalise them unfairly.

△ Former President George Bush of the United States (centre) at talks with the former Soviet president, Mikhail Gorbachev (right), in Malta, December 1989. At this summit Gorbachev proposed an international conference to discuss the future of Europe.

The future

There are many social, political and economic issues facing the community in the future. One problem is that of attempted immigration into Europe. Britain faces urgent demands from millions of citizens of its Far Eastern colony of Hong Kong to give them rights to British citizenship – and, by extension, to the European Community. Hong Kong people are worried about communist repressions when the People's Republic of China repossesses the territory in the year 1997. Another problem is the protection of the environment. Centuries of industrial expansion and urban growth have polluted Europe's rivers and destroyed the countryside. The Alps, for example, are under threat from too many tourists.

The Maastricht treaty is certainly an attempt to set Europe on the road towards unity, though Denmark and Britain have expressed reservations about belonging to a "United States of Europe" and a reluctance to pass over control of their currency and budget to Europe. Denmark, having agreed a formula at the Edinburgh Summit in December 1992, is now exempt from key aims of the Maastricht treaty on political and monetary union. Having opted out of a single currency and a common defence policy, a "yes" vote to the Maastricht treaty is expected in Denmark in 1993. With ratification in the British parliament, the Maastricht treaty could come into force by July 1 1993. Compromises in Edinburgh also gave the green light to a rapid enlargement of the EC. The first four applicants – Austria, Finland, Norway and Sweden – are expected to join in 1995. In 1996, the Community will prepare to embrace any other Western European states still outside, and the first wave of the East Europeans.

The events since 1989 in Eastern Europe have altered the political and economic map beyond the EC boundaries. The hope of democratic government and freer trade in this wider arena increase the chances of peace and prosperity for all the citizens of Europe.

▽ In 1989 Hong Kong protesters took to the streets. They were worried about what would happen to the 5.7 million inhabitants of Britain's Far Eastern colony when it is handed over to communist China in 1997. Hong Kong people want British citizenship, which would give them the freedom to live and work anywhere in Europe after 1992.

▷ Jacques Delors is the president of the European Commission. In 1989 he caused a stir by urging members of the EC to move more rapidly towards monetary union. He also wants greater progress to political union.

The European Community

The European Community is made up of 12 independent states, each with its own government. It has 320 million people speaking nine different official languages. Despite their cultural and historical differences, they have all voted to join together to live in peace. They want to work together to improve their standard of living and give Europe a bigger say in world affairs than if they remained separate. The peoples of Europe have fought each other for centuries but now they are determined to settle differences by peaceful negotiation and to strive for more justice and prosperity.

Belgium is a small, flat, prosperous country with a short (66 km) coastline stretching along the North Sea. Almost 47 per cent of its land surface is used for agriculture and 20 per cent is forest. Coal is mined in two large centres. The capital city is Brussels, headquarters of the European Commission. Belgium is a parliamentary democracy with a hereditary monarchy. Legislative power is shared by the king, the Chamber of Representatives and the Senate. The official languages are Flemish and French. German is spoken by a minority in the East. The population is 9.9 million.

Denmark has an area of 43,080 sq km. Although 66 per cent of the land is used for agriculture, it has increasingly valuable oil and natural gas deposits in the North Sea. The capital is Copenhagen. The national language is Danish, although a minority in the south speak German. Almost all Danes belong to the established Evangelical-Lutheran Church. Major exports are foodstuffs, furniture and clothing, machinery and chemicals. Denmark produces food for 5 million people. Denmark is a constitutional monarchy and a parliamentary democracy.

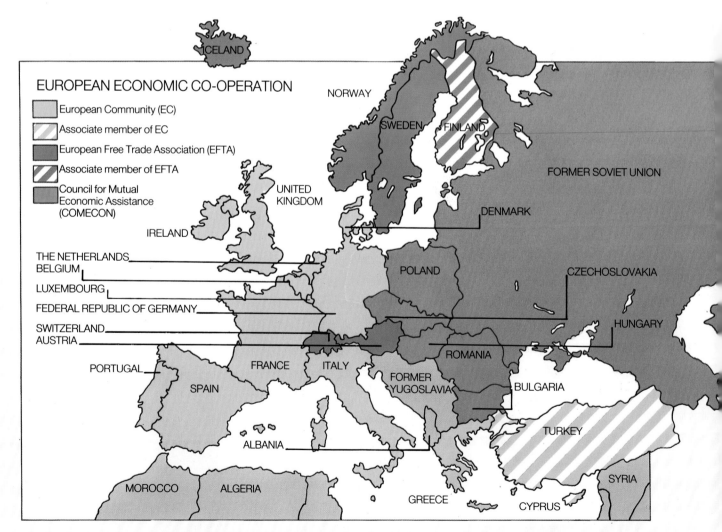

EUROPEAN ECONOMIC CO-OPERATION

- European Community (EC)
- Associate member of EC
- European Free Trade Association (EFTA)
- Associate member of EFTA
- Council for Mutual Economic Assistance (COMECON)

Federal Republic of Germany
Covers an area of about 357,000 sq kilometres. Until 1990, part of Germany was sealed off behind the Iron Curtain which divided Europe. The Federal Republic of Germany (FRG) is the richest country in the community. Now, the cost of bringing in her former Eastern bloc "lande" – administrative areas – is putting great pressure on the economy. The German capital is Berlin and the country has a population of over 78 million. It is a democratic parliamentary state with a federal constitution. It has a head of state and a chancellor who is the head of the federal government. A small minority in the north speak Danish.

France with an area of 544,000 sq km is the largest country in the community, with a population of 55.6 million whose official language is French. Some 58 per cent of the land is used for agriculture. Almost all French citizens are Roman Catholics. France is a republic in which power is shared between the president, the government and the parliament. The capital of France is Paris.

Greece has 2,000 islands in a total land area of 131,990 sq km. Some 75 per cent of the land is used for agriculture, which, together with tourism and shipping make up its principal industries. Greece has 9.9 million inhabitants, most of whom belong to the Greek Orthodox church. Greece is a parliamentary democracy with a president and prime minister.

Ireland lies to the furthest northwest of the community and has a land area of 68,900 sq km. It is a very rural country. Some 95 per cent of the population of 3.5 million are Roman Catholic. Ireland is a parliamentary democracy with a president and a prime minister. The capital is Dublin.

Italy has an area of 301,046 sq km. The capital is Rome and the national language of the population of 57.1 million is Italian. Most Italians are Roman Catholics. Italy is a parliamentary republic. The president is elected by parliament and he appoints a prime minister.

Luxembourg is a small country – only 2,586 sq km. The capital city is also called Luxembourg, and is home to the European Community's Court of Justice. The population is 366,000 with a high proportion of foreigners (26 per cent). "Letzeburgesch" is the national language. Luxembourg is a centre for banking and international business. Some 95 per cent of the population are Roman Catholics, and they are ruled by a grand duke and a chamber of deputies.

The Netherlands has an area of 41,160 sq km, lying very low – more than half below sea level. The biggest city is Amsterdam although the seat of government is at The Hague. With a population of 14.5 million, it is the most densely populated country in the world at 349 inhabitants per acre. The Netherlands is a parliamentary democracy with a queen.

Portugal has a long – 837 km – Atlantic coastline and a total land area of 92,100 sq km. The capital is Lisbon and the national language of the 10.2 million inhabitants is Portuguese. Most Portuguese are Roman Catholics. Although the land is heavily wooded (48 per cent) nearly all the rest of the land is used for agriculture. Portugal exports textiles as well as machinery, pulp and paper, wood and cork and foodstuffs. It is a parliamentary republic.

Spain has an area of 504,800 sq km. There are 39.6 million inhabitants and the official language is Spanish. The predominant religion is Roman Catholicism and its capital is Madrid. Tourism is very important for Spain's economy. Spain is a constitutional monarchy with a parliament. The king is head of state and commander-in-chief of the armed forces.

United Kingdom has an area of 244,111 sq km, mainly consisting of England, Scotland and Wales. A fourth part of the country, Ulster, is in Northern Ireland. Some 77 per cent of the land is used for agriculture and coal and iron ore are mined. The capital is London and the population 56.6 million. Most British people belong to the Anglican or Protestant churches, but in Northern Ireland about 35 per cent of the population is Roman Catholic. Britain is a parliamentary democracy with a queen. The UK has high technology industries and services, including financial ones centred in the City of London.

The EC economy

The economy of Europe, although devastated by the Second World War, is now one of the strongest in the world. Europe has been industrialised for two centuries. In the last 25 years Europeans have doubled their income, having twice as many goods and services at their disposal as they had in 1965. This compares with an increase of only 60 per cent in the United States and an increase of 400 per cent in Japan. However, US income is still higher than European income.

Wealth
Community income is measured in ECUs – European Currency Units, based on the average exchange rate for various European currencies on the world markets. The ecu is currently worth about 60 pence.

The total combined Gross Domestic Product (GDP) of the European 12 was 3,314 million ecus in 1985 compared with Japan's 1,754 million and the United States's massive 5,172 million.

Within the community there are great differences both within and between countries. The regions of Extremadura within Spain and Limousin within France are comparatively poor. Luxembourg, Denmark and the Federal Republic of Germany (FRG) as a whole are rich compared with Spain, Greece and Portugal.

Agriculture
Under the proposed terms of the Common Agricultural Policy (CAP) reform, community subsidies to agriculture will be reduced by 15 per cent. This reform accords with the requirement of the Uruguay round of the GATT talks. However, it has already caused unrest amongst the community's farmers, who have seen their livelihoods dwindle and land taken out of production in recent times. Community subsidies to farmers, it is argued, cause the burden of inflated food prices to fall unfairly upon consumers, especially the poor, who spend nearly 40 per cent of their budget on food. Also, producers in Third World countries cannot compete on equal terms with the protected EC farmers. Owing to the CAP, the community has had embarassing and unwanted surpluses of commodities such as butter and meat, wine and oil.

Energy
The community produces more than half the energy it consumes, but that still means that it is heavily dependent on importing such commodities as oil and gas. There are five sources of primary energy: oil, coal, natural gas, nuclear energy and hydroelectricity. Oil is the community's main source of energy supply (45 per cent) and nuclear energy is very important in France, where it provides 70 per cent of energy.

Industry
Europe depends to a large extent on external sources for its raw materials. It imports nearly all its copper, iron ore, phosphates and nickel. Once a major world producer of iron and steel, ships and cars, Europe now has booming service industries. Transport, banking, tourism and medical care are some examples of services. This move from heavy and manufacturing industry to services is sometimes called "post-industrial" economy. For a while the transition process had a drastic effect on European levels of employment, since more than 4 million jobs were lost from old industries.

Europe and the Third World
Some 3,700 million people live in the Third World. Their average annual income is only 920 ecus a year, compared with European 9,300 ecus. Europe feels a responsibility to help Third World countries develop their economies. Europeans developed trade with many territories during the period of European colonial expansion. Having regained their independence, these countries continue to supply raw materials to Europe. Aid is sent from Europe to enable the poorer countries of the world to industrialise and develop in an attempt to correct the imbalance in this economic relationship.

Other external trade
The European Community is the leading trading power in the world, accounting for nearly 20 per cent of world trade. By 1986, more than half the EC's total imports were of manufactured goods. The community's main suppliers are the United States and the EFTA countries comprising Norway, Sweden, Finland, Austria and Switzerland. The community has a balance of trade surplus with the rest of the world.

The Maastricht treaty

The Maastricht treaty aims to effect economic and monetary union (EMU) and to establish a new framework for European Union. Critics of Maastricht argue that the treaty effectively gives more power to the European Parliament in Brussels and may result in a United States of Europe.

Subsidiarity aims to define the nature and direction of power in the European Community (EC). The terms of the treaty are as follows:

 All EC countries except Britain will be bound by the EC law regarding workers hours and pay.

 All citizens of the EC will become "citizens of the European Union". EC nationals living in another EC country will have the right to vote and stand in municipal and European elections.

 European defence will be consolidated around the existing Western European Union (WEU) which gained credibility during the Gulf War.

 A single Euro-currency will be created at the latest by January 1999, at the earliest by 1995. A single European bank independent of political influence will manage the EC money and economy.

 Euro-MP's will have the right to veto national laws in 14 different fields including public health and culture.

New community powers are introduced in the fields of education, public health, culture, consumer protection. major trans-frontier infrastructure projects, such as roads and bridges and research and industry. Majority voting rather than unanimity and the right of national veto is substituted in many areas.

The Maastricht treaty establishes a new framework for European Union, resting on three so-called "pillars" of cooperation under the European Council;

1. The European Community – governed by the Treaty of Rome, the Single European Act and the Maastricht treaty;

2. Common Foreign and Security Policy – as agreed between national governments according to the Maastricht treaty;

3. Justice and Home Affairs, also to be decided by intergovernmental cooperation as laid down in the Maastricht treaty.

Subsidiarity
The concept of subsidiarity as it appears in the Maastricht treaty is open to various interpretations. Claimed to be a safeguard against federalism, it lays down clear limits to the power of EC institutions for those who are worried about the erosion of the power of the member states. Transparency is Euro-speak for opening up the secretive decision-making institutions of the Community.

The EC administration

Like the United Nations and the British Commonwealth, the European Community is an effort to build a just, peaceful and prosperous world. However the European Community is unique because, while each member state so far has kept its independence and autonomy, common institutions have been created where proposals can be discussed and decisions made for the benefit of all.

The Council of Ministers

The Council of 12 ministers, one from each member state, is the decision-making body of the community. The council is chaired in turn by each member state for six months. For instance, for the first half of 1990 the chair is held by Ireland, in the second half by Italy, then the Netherlands .

The European Commission

The Commission proposes community legislation to the Council. There are 17 members of the Commission, each appointed for four years. They are not there to represent their own country's interests, but those of the community as a whole. The president of the European Commission is Jacques Delors, who will see Europe through to 1992.

The European Parliament

The European Parliament has grown in importance since 1979, when members were first elected by direct universal adult suffrage. The 518 members are elected for five years and they group together on the basis of political tendency rather than nationality. Parliament's job is to watch over the budget and the operation of the work of the commission. It intervenes in the law-making process and can sack the commission.

The new co-operation procedure 1986

Under the new procedure the Council of Ministers does not have the final say on any new EC law. Parliament has the right to amend or reject the Council's position on a new law if a majority of its members agree to this. The council may then adopt a new law if there is a majority for it.

The European Commission

It proposes any new laws and then takes parliament's opinion before submitting it to the Council.

▽ The European Community headquarters in Brussels. It houses all the committees and administration of the EC. The European Parliament sits in Strasbourg in France.

The Court of Justice

interprets all EC laws and acts independently. Anyone can bring a case against his or her government to this Court.

The European Parliament

watches over the working of the Commission and discusses new laws. Elections to it are held every five years.

The Council of Ministers

is composed of ministers from the 12 member states. It is the decision-making body of the EC.

The Court of Justice

The Court of Justice of the European Communities is based in Luxembourg. Its task is to interpret the European Constitution and the application of community laws. It has 13 judges, one from each country plus one to make an odd number.

Other EC bodies

Other European Community bodies include: the Economic and Social Committee, based in Brussels; the Commission is bound to consult its 189 members, who represent employers, trade unions and consumers, on proposals relating to economic and social matters; the Court of Auditors who monitor the spending of European revenues; the European Investment Bank, which lends money for capital projects to help the community grow; the European Bank for Reconstruction and Development (EBRD) which was set up in 1990 to foster the transition of countries in central and eastern Europe to market-orientated economies; and GATT which is a world trading watchdog, overseeing trade between 102 countries around the world.

The Common Agricultural Policy (CAP)

was begun in 1962. It provides subsidies for community food. For the last four years, support prices to the farmer have dropped by 10 per cent. However, support for farmers is a sensitive political and social issue in the community which has 10 million farmers compared with only 3.8 million in the United States and five million in Japan.

The European Agricultural Guidance and Guarantee Fund

looks after Europe's forests. In fact Europe has only four per cent of the world's forest resources and 172 million ecus is being spent on projects to improve timber stocks.

The Common Fisheries Policy

protects stocks of fish within community waters and deals with the interests of the fishing industry.

The European Space Agency

trains between 40 and 50 graduates a year in its Horizon 2000 programme in the Netherlands.

The Cohesion Fund

Set up under Maastricht to enable poorer countries to catch up with their richer neighbours.

The Western European Union

(WEU) was formed in 1954, following the 1948 Treaty of Brussels. Members must be in NATO and are; Belgium, Britain, France, Germany, Italy, Luxembourg, the Netherlands, Spain and Portugal. The organisation gained credibility during the 1991 Gulf War when 5 EC members sent naval forces under a WEU initiative.

The Social Fund

gives financial help to training and employment schemes, particularly in areas of high unemployment, for young people and for the disabled.

The Regional Development Fund

was set up in 1975 to help parts of the EC situated in difficult geographical areas or areas of high unemployment. Further guarantees of job security, minimum wages and worker participation in the running of industry are envisaged in the "Social Charter", proposed for discussion by the president of the European Commission, Jacques Delors. Work is also in progress on the harmonisation of standards – from medical qualifications to light bulbs, in order to make EC living a reality.

Chronology

490 BC Battle of Marathon – a Greek victory against the Persians which opened the greatest age of Greece and saw the birth of democracy and European civilisation.

5 BC Birth of Jesus of Nazareth, founder of the Christian religion.

117 AD Roman Empire at its height.

410 Sack of Rome by Alaric the Goth followed by waves of barbarian invasions.

793 onwards: Viking raids on Europe including Seville (844).

800 Charlemagne crowned emperor.

1066-1100 Norman conquest of Britain, Italy and Sicily.

1215 Magna Carta, signed by English King John at Runnymede. Sets out legal limits to the power of the monarch for the first time.

1264 First Oxford College founded by Walter de Merton. By 1400 there would be 53 European universities.

1450-55 Gutenburg invents printing. First bible printed.

1453 Constantinople falls to the Turks. Beginning of the Renaissance.

1492 Reconquest of Spain by Ferdinand and Isabella from the Arabs; Christopher Columbus sets sail for the New World and discovers the Americas.

1517 Luther initiates the Reformation.

1519-1522 Ferdinand Magellan circumnavigates the globe.

1536-39 Dissolution of the monasteries by English King Henry VIII.

1643-1715 Louis XIV is king of France.

1789 The French Revolution is followed by the Terror and civil war.

1848 Revolutions in France, Italy, Germany, Hungary and Bohemia.

1870-71 Franco-Prussian war.

1914-18 First World War.

1939-45 Second World War.

1951 European Coal and Steel Community formed (Treaty of Paris).

1957 Treaties of Rome create the European Economic Community and Euratom.

1962 Common Agricultural Policy agreed.

1963 First Yaoundé Convention with 17 African countries.

1963 Turkey becomes an associate member of the EC.

1969 Second Yaoundé Convention.

1972 United Kingdom, Ireland and Denmark join the original Six.

1975 First Lomé Convention takes place with 46 ACP countries.

1979 First direct elections to European Parliament; creation of European Monetary System; second Lomé Convention with 66 ACP countries.

1981 Greece joins. Ecu formally adopted as European unit of account.

1984 Second direct elections to European Parliament.

1986 Spain and Portugal join. First European passports issued. Signing of the Single European Act.

1989 Communist governments fall in Poland, Hungary, East Germany, Czechoslovakia, Bulgaria and Romania.

1990 Unification of Germany as Berlin wall dismantled.

1991 The Soviet Union is dissolved. The Gulf War provokes unease that German troops were unable to support their European allies in the field due to the article in their constitution limiting their operations to NATO territory.

1991 Heads of government agree the terms of the Treaty of Maastricht.

1992 The Danes vote "no" to Maastricht; the French (narrowly) and the Irish vote "yes". Switzerland votes "no" to joining the EEA.

1992 The Edinburgh Summit debates a strategy to pull the EC out of deepening recession and regains Danish support for the Maastricht treaty after an opt-out clause is introduced.

Glossary

Autonomy is when a person or body is independent and not subject to interference from outside.

Capitalism is the economic system in which most enterprises are owned privately. Wealth or capital can be put to whatever use the individual wants.

Catholic is short for Roman Catholic and is the part of the Christian church headed by the Pope in Rome.

Christianity is the religion started by Jesus of Nazareth. Members of the Christian church believe that Jesus was the son of God.

Communism is the belief that all private wealth should be abolished and all things are held in common, that is, by the state. In practice the state decides who has money and fixes prices.

Democracy is the system of government where the people regularly elect representatives in a secret ballot from among several political parties.

Ecu stands for economic currency unit. Its value is fixed in relation to a basket of set amounts of other community currencies.

EMS stands for European Monetary System. It came into existence on 12 March 1979. The ecu is the central element of the EMS. Not all EC countries participate fully in the EMS. Greece, Spain, Portugal and the United Kingdom do not.

ERM stands for Exchange Rate Mechanism. It is designed to help European trade by getting rid of extreme changes in the exchange rate of currencies. Central banks agree to support a currency which is in trouble.

European Commission has 17 members and proposes community laws to the Council of Ministers. It supervises the day-to-day running of those policies.

European Parliament Every five years EC electors choose their Members of the European Parliament (MEPs). The parliament has 518 members with a secretariat in Luxembourg. It sits in Strasbourg and has committee meetings in Brussels.

First World War was fought from 1914-18. It was the first of two great European wars in the 20th century. The Allies (Britain, France, Russia and later Italy and the United States) fought the Central Powers (Germany, the Austro-Hungarian Empire joined by Turkey). The Allies won and it resulted in the setting up of many smaller nation states in Central and Eastern Europe.

NATO the North Atlantic Treaty Organisation was founded in 1949. It is an alliance between 16 democracies: Belgium, Canada, Denmark, Federal Republic of Germany, France, Greece, Iceland, Italy, Luxembourg, the Netherlands, Norway, Portugal, Spain, Turkey, United Kingdom and the United States.

Nationalism is the enthusiasm for one's country or nation. It became a factor in world politics from 1500 onwards.

Parliament is the body of elected representatives, which meets to propose and discuss new laws, agree on taxes and govern a country.

Protestantism is the movement of Christians who broke away from the Roman Catholic church in the 16th century.

Second World War lasted from 1939-45. It was fought between the Axis powers (Germany, Italy and Japan) and the Allies (the United States, the Soviet Union, Britain, France and others). It ended with the defeat of Japan and Germany and the division of Europe.

Single European Act was signed by the 12 in 1986. It agreed to achieve an open market without barriers within the community by 1992.

Treaties of Rome established the European Economic Community (EEC) and the European Atomic Energy Community (Euratom). They were signed in March 1957 by the Six – France, Federal Republic of Germany, Italy, Belgium, the Netherlands and Luxembourg.

Warsaw Pact is a defence treaty agreeing to mutual military assistance, signed by the Soviet Union, Poland, Czechoslovakia, the German Democratic Republic, Hungary Romania and Bulgaria.

Index

absolutism 9, 10
ACP countries 25
Africa 8, 25
agriculture 3, 18, 21, 28, 30, 33
associate status 18, 25
Atlantic Alliance 17
atomic bomb 13
Austria 11, 24
Azerbaijanis 23

Belgium 3, 16, 21, 28
Berlin Wall 16
British Commonwealth 17, 32
broadcasting 20, 33
Brussels 28, 32, 33
Bush, George 26

Canada 14
capitalism 3, 4, 35
Caribbean 8, 25
Catholic workers' party 23
Channel Tunnel 24
Charlemagne 6
China 8, 14, 27
Christianity 4-7, 9, 11, 35
Churchill, Winston 16
co-operation procedure 20, 32
Cohesion Fund 33
Cold War 13, 16
colonialism 9-11, 25, 27
Columbus, Christopher 8, 9
Common Agricultural Policy (CAP) 18, 33
Common European bank 19, 27
Common Fisheries Policy 33
communism 11, 13, 16, 22, 23, 26, 27, 35
Council of Ministers 3, 17, 19, 20, 32, 33, 35
Court of Auditors 33
Court of Justice 17, 33
Czechoslovakia 23

De Gaulle, General Charles 18, 19
defence 16, 17, 26
Delors, Jacques 27, 32, 33
democracy 3-5, 7, 10, 13, 15, 19, 22, 23, 28, 35
Denmark 3, 18, 19, 21, 28, 30
direct elections 19, 32, 33

East Germany 13, 16, 22
Eastern Europe 11, 13, 16, 22, 23, 26, 27, 30
economic aid 23, 25, 26, 31
Economic and Social Committee 33
economic integration 17, 18, 24
economy 30
ecus 19, 20, 30, 31, 35
Edinburgh 3, 27, 34
Einstein, Albert 10
empires 4, 11, 12, 17, 30
energy 19, 30
Ethiopia 25
European Agricultural Guidance and Guarantee Fund 33
European Atomic Energy Committee (Euratom) 17, 35
European Coal and Steel Community (ECSC) 14, 15, 16, 17
European Commission 17, 20, 21, 27, 28, 32, 33, 35
European Community 2-4, 13, 15, 19, 24, 27, 28
European Constitution 33
European Economic Community (EEC) 17, 18, 19, 35
European Investment Bank 23, 33
European Monetary System (EMS) 19, 35
European Parliament 3, 17, 19-21, 32, 33, 35
European Space Agency 33
Exchange Rate Mechanism (ERM) 19, 35

feudal system 7, 10
First World War 11, 12, 14, 16, 35
France 3, 5-7, 9-12, 14-19, 21, 22, 24, 27, 29, 30
French Revolution 10

German Democratic Republic 16, 29
Germany 2, 3, 5-7, 11-16, 18, 21, 23, 26, 27, 29, 30
Gonzales, Felipe 19
Gorbachev, Mikhail 22, 26

Greece 3-5, 18, 19, 21, 29, 30
guaranteed prices 18, 25, 30, 33

harmonisation 18, 33
humanism 4, 9
Hungary 16, 23

immigration 27
industrial revolution 10
industry 3, 20, 21, 30
Ireland 3, 18, 19, 21, 29, 32
Islam 7, 9
Israel 25
Italy 3, 5, 7, 11, 12, 16, 17, 20, 21, 29, 30, 32

Japan 30, 33
Joan of Arc 7

Krenz, Egon 22

language 3, 28, 29
law 5, 20, 32, 33
League of Nations 14
Lomé Conventions 25
Luxembourg 3, 14, 16, 21, 29, 30, 32, 33

markets 18, 24, 25
Maastricht 2, 3, 27, 31, 34
Marx, Karl 10, 11, 35
Members of the European Parliament (MEPs) 19, 35
Middle Ages 7
monetary union 27
Monnet, Jean 13-16
Morocco 25, 27

nation states 7, 11
national security 26
nationalism 12, 24, 35
Netherlands 3, 9, 16, 21, 29, 32, 33
North Atlantic Treaty Organisation (NATO) 17, 26, 35

Pétain, Marshal Henri-Philippe 14
Poland 13, 14, 16, 23, 27
political union 18, 19, 24, 27
pollution 27
Pompidou, Georges 18
population 3, 25, 28

Portugal 3, 8, 19, 21, 29, 30
Protestants 9, 35

raw materials 10, 11, 25, 30
Reformation 4, 9
Regional Development Fund 33
religion 4-7, 9, 29, 35
Renaissance 4, 8, 38
Roman Catholics 9, 35
Rome 4-6, 9, 10
Russian Revolution 11

Schuman, Robert 16
Second World War 2, 12-14, 16, 23, 26, 30, 35
Single European Act 20, 35
single market 3, 20, 24, 26
"Social Charter" 33
Social Fund 33
Solidarnosc (Solidarity) 22
sovereignty 14, 16, 27
Soviet Union 3, 6, 11, 13, 16, 17, 22-23
Spain 3, 5, 7, 9, 19, 21, 29, 30
surpluses 30, 33
Sweden 14, 24
Switzerland 24

technology 4, 10, 27
Third World 25, 31
tourism 27, 31
trade 3, 7, 18, 19, 24, 30, 35
transport 18, 24, 30
Treaties of Rome 17, 18, 26, 27, 35
Turkey 18, 25, 27

United Kingdom 3, 6, 7, 9-12, 14, 16-19, 21, 24, 26, 27, 29
United Nations 32
United States 3, 10, 12-14, 16, 17, 24, 26, 30, 33
United States of Europe 15, 16, 27

Warsaw Pact 17, 35
Western civilisation 4-6, 9, 11
Western European Union 33

Yeltsin, Boris 22, 23
Yugoslavia 7, 23

Photographic Credits:
Front cover and page 23 both: Frank Spooner Pictures; pages 2-3, 8 middle, 18, 18-19, 20-21, 22 bottom, 24 bottom, 26-27 & 27 bottom: Topham Picture Source; 7, 16-17, 21 & 31: J. Allan Cash Library; page 4-5: Werner Forman Archive; pages 6, 8 top & bottom & 10: Mary Evans Picture Library; 9: Robert Harding Picture Library; 12 top: Hulton Deutsch; 12 bottom & 13 both: Popperfoto: 16: Monnet Archive; 24-25: Hutchison Library; back cover: Roger Vlitos.